kenzie

HarperCollins*Publishers*

77–85 Fulham Palace Road, Hammersmith, London W6 8JB

www.harpercollins.co.uk

Published by HarperCollins*Entertainment* 2005

1 3 5 7 9 8 6 4 2

Copyright © James Mackenzie 2005

The Author asserts the moral right to be identified as the author of this work

A catalogue record for this book is available from the British Library

ISBN 0 00 721149 X

Designed by Butler and Tanner
Set in Futura and Handel Gothic

Printed and bound in Great Britain by Butler and Tanner

Photographs: © Alan Strutt/www.celebritypictures.co.uk 33, 65, 97, 101, 119;
© Alpha Press 43; © Big Pictures 36, 37, 49; © Bravado International Group Ltd
19, 60, 62, 71, 73, 74, 77, 78, 81, 82, 85, 86, 90; © Capital Pictures 103;
© Ellis Parrinder/Camera Press 56; © Empics 6 (bottom left & right), 47, 59, 95,
127; © Famous 125; © Jamie Baker/Camera Press 98; © John Murray 40, 44,
51, 53, 54-55, 92; © London Features International 68, 69, 89; © Retna 57, 94;
© Rex Features 104, 106, 109, 111, 113, 114, 116; © Rowen Laurence/Famous
29; © Soccer Six Official Photography 16, 21, 24 (bottom)

kenzie

Harper
Collins

For my Mum, Dad and Brother, John

Thank you to Albert Samuel, David Samuel,
Amy Styles and Elliot Blackmore at ASM Ltd.
Gary Howard and Richard Smith at Mission Control.
Alexis Grower at Magrath & Co.
All at Ross Bennet Smith. Mark Sutton, Kevin Holly and Tony Cave.
All the Blazin Boys and all my family – too many to mention!

I would also like to thank Martin Roach, who collaborated with me on this book.

Contents

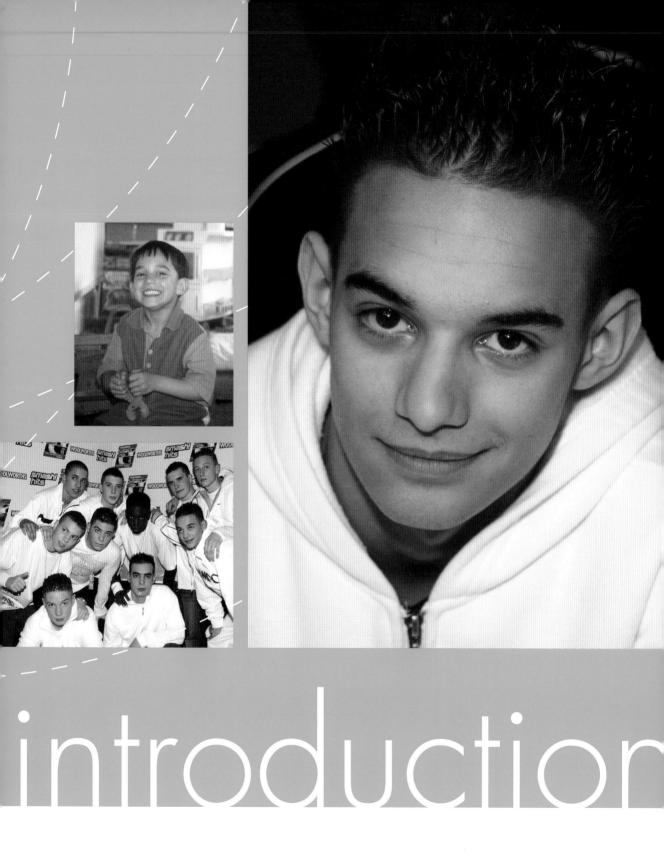

introduction

kenzie

I am sitting on a chair opposite Sylvester Stallone's mother. She is in her seventies, I am nineteen. About eight million people are watching us talk.

'So, who are you again?' she says.

'My name is Kenzie and I am a rapper in a band.'

'A band? What do you mean, a band?'

'There's ten of us, we call ourselves Blazin' Squad.'

'What sort of band ...?'

'You know, like 50 Cent, Eminem, what they do, but not as good!'

'What, you mean like breakdancing?'

'No! Not at all like breakdancing!'

I pause for a moment, taking in the craziness of my situation. I haven't seen my family for days. I haven't heard music for days. I am talking to Rambo's mum about music. And you know what? I love it ...

How did I get here?

This is how it happened ...

1

sofas and studios

Both my parents have been instrumental in me being able to pursue music as a career. My dad was brought up in Watford and when he was young used to make rubbish money labouring. My mum grew up in County Tyrone in a little town called Benburb; we still have family there and I go out and watch the Gaelic football with them.

Mum and Dad have always been teachers. Mum's a Deputy Head and really intelligent. She's fluent in Spanish and can teach English, maths, everything; she's pretty multi-talented. Dad's Head of Humanities at a nearby girls' school.

Neither Mum nor Dad were musicians. They both listened to music, Dad more than Mum but they didn't play (I briefly had piano lessons around the age of five). Having said that, I do have vivid memories of my dad chasing me around our sofa while REM's 'Losing My Religion' played in the background. To this day that is one of my all-time favourite tunes. Whenever I turn on

9

kenzie

MTV and that song is playing, it brings that memory flooding back.

I was born on 6 January 1986. The years when I was very young I just remember a feeling of being really well looked after. There was so much love for me. We lived in a flat in Walthamstow, near to my childhood home, for the first six weeks of my life but I don't remember this at all. Then we moved to a house in Highams Park, which is where we still live.

The way my parents have brought me up is always to be polite – 'first impressions count' – and that's helped so much in the music industry, remembering what they

told me. I am half-Indian from my dad's side and with my mum coming from Northern Ireland I'm quite an unusual mix, which is nice. It's good to be a bit different.

My brother, John, is quite shy. He's three years younger than me. We used to fight a lot when we were growing up, but since all the music stuff kicked off we've got a much stronger relationship. We didn't always see eye to eye, but now he's more confident and we can have a laugh and play-fight – he's waiting for the day he is taller than me; he keeps saying, 'I'll come back for you!'

He is a little musical genius. I bought a studio for him and he's into the production – we do work together. He definitely wants to get into music. I think he's got his heart set on it and, by the way I am going on, I can help to give him that opportunity. We bought that studio when he was fourteen and already he is making beats for my band, sending beats to my management and stuff like that. It's nice 'cos we can be on the same wavelength. I've got the connections and the advice to tell him what might happen. I think we will start off a generation of musicians for the family to come.

Although I was lucky enough to be brought up in a good home with a great family, there is one incident that happened to us that is straight out of *The X-Files*. I woke up one morning and walked downstairs to find builders

everywhere. I thought, 'No one told me you were decorating!' Then Mum told me a six-foot block of ice had fallen through the kitchen roof. What?

At six in the morning, this massive slab of ice had smashed through our kitchen ceiling, sliced the dishwasher clean in two and basically demolished everything nearby. There was a huge hole in the roof and mess everywhere. I'd slept through the whole thing. My brother said he thought a wardrobe had fallen over. It was scary; had someone been in the kitchen making a cup of tea or something they could have been killed. They reckoned it had fallen from about 20,000 feet but we never found out who was responsible. I think my mum has still got some of the ice. It obviously needs to be a bigger block to wake me up ...

My primary school years were spent at Handsworth School, which is only a short walk from my house. That backs on to a secondary school which I went to as well, so my education was all mapped out for me from day one. I was quite small and shy back then but I was quite lucky: I didn't get subjected to much bullying. I saw it going on but I was quite sociable and able to get on with people. Besides, I think I was too easy a target! It wasn't a rough school at all; it's just that bullying goes

on everywhere. The first few years there I was very quiet, but then I started hanging around with a group of older boys. I used to walk about the streets with them and we would play football, so I grew up quite quickly with them. There was a boy named Stuart Begg, another called Joe Graham (one of my best friends to this day – we are always together) and a load of others, including Josh Johnson and Mark Cumber. They were all bigger than me, naturally, so they kind of looked out for me too. We went everywhere, swimming, getting up to a bit of mischief. I loved it.

Towards the end of primary school, I developed a bit of cockiness, some cheekiness, and this started to get me into trouble a little. I was quite intimidated by the Head Teacher; she just had this really fierce, you-don't-want-to-go-there sort of look, which had kept me in line for a long time, but then I started to get a bit more confident.

In a way, I think because my parents were teachers, everyone expected me to be this A-star student but I just wanted to perform and put on a show, a bit of fairly harmless attention-seeking really. At school, when it came to music and acting classes I didn't have that much confidence, but if it was just mucking about with my mates, I loved entertaining people.

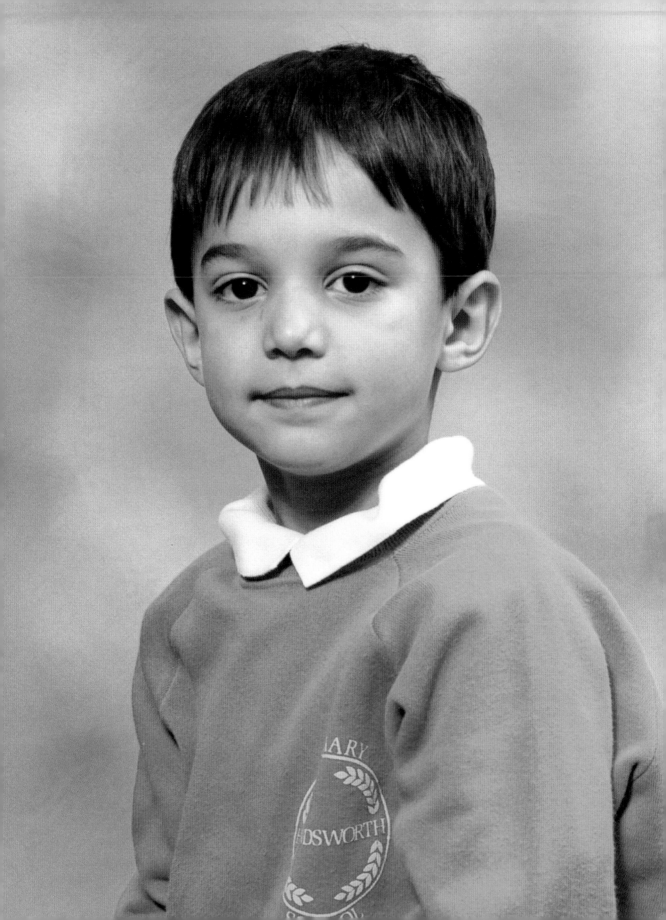

With most of my mates being from the year above, when they left I went a bit mad. They were all starting their new life in secondary school and I was still on the other side of the fence in primary school. I felt so isolated. Friends from those times tell me I flipped, and I look back now and regret my behaviour. I was rude to people and very stuck up and I did get into trouble. Teachers would say stuff to me and I would really argue and give them backchat. I wasn't bothered about any class unless it was PE; I just wanted to play football and run around like a madman. I just loved showing off and trying to impress people but that didn't always do me any favours at school. Eventually, letters were sent home to my parents and it reached a low point when they had to go into school to discuss my behaviour.

But then I started to become closer friends with people in my own year. One boy – I had actually been to nursery school with him and we'd played a lot of football together – was Stuart Baker, who would later be Reepa in Blazin' Squad.

the decks,
the stations,
the garage

The first record I ever bought was Coolio's 'Gangsta's Paradise'. I'd heard it on the radio and loved it. I didn't have a clue about the whole gangsta rap culture but I just loved the sound. 'Mo' Money Mo' Problems' by Biggie was another tune I bought early on. Tupac's 'Changes' hit me big time one Saturday morning when it came on the telly and to this day it is still one of the best songs I have ever heard. That hit me down the rap route very early on.

I listen back now and laugh 'cos these artists would be rapping about all these ghetto issues and I'd think I knew what they were saying, but I'd be way off the mark! But it ain't about that at that age. You're picking up on a head beat, a good hook, you can act the lyrics and try to copy them. You don't look up to them all seriously as role models – they are probably the last people your parents would want as a role model; you just see these men performing and entertaining and doing their thing. It was all about the vibe.

I was just going wherever my ears took me. I also bought Oasis's *(What's The Story) Morning Glory?* But that was about it for me and Britpop. I was quite into Oasis but Britpop meant nothing to me. I was only ten. I later found out that Blur used Walthamstow Dog Track, a stone's throw from my house, for the artwork and promotion of their big *Parklife* album, but at the time I was completely oblivious to this. I was into Californian gangsta rappers and, later, underground garage.

It seems funny now knowing what we have done with Blazin' Squad, but way back in late primary school I went down to the park one day and there, sitting on a bench, were three kids who would go on to become fellow band members: Melo, Flava and Spike-E. They were from a different primary school but no one bothered about that. I was with my mates, Jordan and Steve, and we all got chatting and started to hang out together.

Before music, the common bond was football. We played for New Forest Rangers, which was run by my best mate Stuart's dad, Martin Winter. It was almost a Blazin' Squad XI: there was Reepa, Freek, Krazy, Flava, Melo-D, Mus and myself. That was a great social thing to do and we were all well into it.

On my first day at Highams Park Secondary School I was just following my older mates around; I didn't know what to do. I mixed with that group of boys and the ones from my own year too, which was nice. I was really tight at the time with my mate Stuart Winter; we used to go everywhere together – Center Parcs, all over the place. It didn't take me long to get involved in the whole business of 'looking right' at school. You had to have the right bag, cool shoes, you couldn't have your top button done up, you couldn't have jack ups (where your trousers are too short in the leg). If you didn't have all the right gear, people picked up on it and you thought your life was over. Now I think I should have just been myself but at that age it is so important. Back then, I really still didn't have any confidence, so I was keen to fit in.

I came out of my shell in Year 9, specifically on a school trip to Italy. It was the best holiday of my life and probably always will be. We went to a place called Rio de Jesolo and it was just wicked. I pulled girls, I had a laugh with all the boys, played football on the beach and tried to impress people, and I thought, 'This is what I am all about!' I really came out of myself. That's when it all kicked off for me, after that holiday; it weren't about school, it was about girls and music.

That holiday did so much for me. I got in with such a big group of friends, we were away from everything back home, I could go back to my hotel whenever I wanted, everyone was happy to be in the sun and it brought us all together. My older mates were on the trip as well, which really helped because they'd been before, so I always had someone to look after me. In the photos I'm wearing this XXXL Ralph Lauren shirt that I fell in love with and thought I looked absolutely amazing in!

When we got back home, I got into music, girls and fashion big time. I had a phase of being really into Ben Sherman shirts. That was the thing – a plain Ben Sherman shirt, a pair of pinstripes, and a pair of Ravels. If you looked like that, it was all happening for you, mate; you're under eighteen and you are doing well!

I just wanted to **play music** and **text girls**

I must have had about twenty-five Ben Sherman shirts, which were not cheap. The hip-hop clothing had not kicked off with us yet; that came a lot later for me. It was a little odd because I was listening to hip-hop and starting to listen to garage, but I was wearing a Ben Sherman, which a lot of the Britpop lot wore. So that was a strange mix really. I just wanted to look like everyone else. You usually do at that age.

I wasn't good at school after that holiday; I just wanted to play music and text girls and my parents would always have to remind me to do my homework! That's how I developed my love of music really, because I was rebelling from school so much. I wasn't totally bad – I don't want to come across like I was terrible in school – but I didn't do myself any favours. I didn't wanna be top of the class, so I would actually go out of my way to try and get things wrong. I'd sit in an exam and deliberately make mistakes. I look back on that and feel annoyed with myself, especially because if I'd have been better at English then I'd have had so much more intelligence and that would have fuelled my ability to rap and to write. Nas and Jay-Z use words that I don't even know what they mean … I look back and think I'd write the most amazing song if I'd got an A star in English … but you do what you think is best for you at the time.

The original football group all had other friends and over the years the numbers expanded until eventually it was this massive crowd hanging out together. We used to walk about in groups of about sixty, with loads of girls. That was what we lived for – Friday nights was White Lightning, a laugh, a kebab and a great time. Cheap, great, hilarious stories for the rest of your life.

Despite all this, my mum and dad were really lenient and they still looked out for me so amazingly. For my thirteenth Christmas they bought me a set of decks. Plus, they would let me blast it out; I never had any complaints. It wasn't as if they knew I was going to be famous; they'd just let me blast it out. Obviously, at first I was appalling. I didn't know what to do so I rang my mate Mark Cumber (who's not actually in Blazin' Squad) and we got into it big time. No one I knew wanted a guitar or a drum kit; it was all about the decks.

Those decks were all I ever wanted, they just looked so smart. They were Electrovison & Newmark, not a big name at all, but they were direct-drive decks rather than belt drives, so I was spoilt (a direct drive really helps when you are scratching in the beat and they are substantially more expensive than belt drives). My dad's youngest brother, Uncle Glynne, explained the difference

kenzie

to me. He was on the music side of things so we relate, and when I look at him I see myself, the cheekiness, that proper, entertaining-the-family streak, but I also see a reflection of my dad too, half and half. He was quite musical at the time and had a set of Technics 12-10s, which were my all-time dream decks.

I used to make tapes all the time. I had a stereo but we didn't plug it in direct. We just all had to be quiet, then I'd press a button; I couldn't take any phone calls and my mum and dad couldn't shout upstairs, while I'd put the stereo next to the decks and it would pick the tape up from the decks. It was the worst quality but the most pleasure listening to yourself when you are only thirteen. The day I got my decks was the day it all started for me. It was a really special day: someone was watching over me.

All my boys got into it as well … I'd be upstairs in my box room and Mum and Dad would let me have seven of my mates in there, all sweaty, thumping the music out down the whole street like a full-on performance … and still they didn't mind! Sometimes, I would even stick my head around the living-room door and say, 'Do you want me to turn it down?,' and they'd say, 'No, no problem, James.'

Them being so lenient made it so easy for me to invite everyone around my house and do what we wanted to do with the music. That's how it started really, that original group of mates coming round mine, mucking about with that first set of decks.

Making tapes – that's what we lived for. It was a good way of socializing, talking about it at the time and at school, and it was cool to be known as the people with decks, early MCs if you like. It gave us a bit more credibility around school. That's all I wanted to do; make a tape, listen to it. I'd pump it up in the morning before I went to school, play it on the Walkman in school and then after school … it was almost a way of being sociable. It brought us all together.

My very first public stint as an MC was a party down the bottom of our road. Someone set their decks up and another school came down and said, 'We wanna battle with you.' By this time, I could do it, I was there, me and the boys were there, so three of us went on stage representing our school (myself, Strider and Plat-Num) and three representing their school. It just blew me away, the way people were taking us; it was such a buzz. I will probably never be able to repeat that buzz, even though we've since played places like Wembley as Blazin' Squad.

I soon developed a name as an MC along with my other boys. I was always called Kenzie; my mate came up with that. When it all first started, we had a crew called the Alongside Crew, before Blazin' Squad, which was me, Flava, a boy called Jason aka Darky, and my mate Marc – he was Kaos – Frank Condon aka Franky C and Mus, who called himself Pussy. That was the original 'box room boys', either at my house or in Marc's loft.

Marc and Jason were older than us and along with Frank they kind of lost interest after a while. Me and Flava carried on doing it, and we could both DJ too. At first we used to be 'Kenzie and Frenzy' (I haven't used my real name, James, for years), but then he changed his name to Flava. Me and Flava used to smoke behind the blue containers at school. One day he said to me, 'Let's start a group called Blazin' Squad.'

I said, 'No, man, we've got the Alongside Crew, we're cool. Blazin' Squad will never work.'

He said, 'Trust me, it will!'

'No, mate, it won't work!'

It did.

Not long after that, we got all the other boys involved. There were five of us: Kenzie, Flava, Freeky, Spike-E and Melo-D. That was the original Blazin' Squad, Year 9; we were only about fourteen. It was really enjoyable to come into school and stand in the playground and be respected for that. Most people didn't actually know my name; they'd just say, 'That's the DJ boy.'

My DJ-ing was taking off. My friend Mark was older than me so he would get the parties and I would just turn up with my records. Mind you, at my very first DJ gig the needle broke! Oh my God, what do you do? I finished the set with just one decent deck, a mixer and a broken deck. No one's going to get you a needle in the middle of a party, so I just had to get on with it! The MC-ing became a bit hair-raising at times – boys would come down from other areas and you'd have to battle them and sometimes it got a bit tense. You'd be thinking, 'Are my decks safe here? Are they gonna get

stolen?' Generally, though, those parties were wicked. We had the most amazing times.

We were all into the same music: straight-up garage. That was the soundtrack to all these parties. I loved garage, proper hardcore garage as well as the party songs, the male vocal and female vocal garage like 'Monster Boy', Shola Ama's 'Imagine', 'Little Bit Of Luck', quality songs that we grew up on. Plus all the stuff by Oxide and Neutrino, So Solid, Pay As You Go, Nasty Crew, all of these people. The first vinyls I ever bought were 'Rewind' by Craig David and 'Little Bit Of Luck' by DJ Luck & MC Neat (I hooked up with them a few years later, which was weird for me). For the moment, hip-hop was forgotten about.

I'd got these decks and we started getting into the pirate radio and garage scene big time. That was the in thing. I hadn't listened to hip-hop for a while, except for a little bit of Tupac, a little bit of Biggie, just singles. I wouldn't ever have thought of buying an album 'cos I didn't understand it back then.

We'd started listening to pirate radio after we got this tape of some shows and I was instantly converted; that was exactly what I wanted to do. I followed all the stations fanatically: Déjà Vu 92.3, Rinse 100.3, Y2K 90.6, Shine 87.9, Raw Mission 90.0. A lot of these stations were just on a council estate somewhere, in an unwanted flat with a transmitter and a group of people chipping a few quid in and doing what they really loved. It was risky, but they loved doing it.

The fact it was pirate radio made it more appealing … I would never be tuning into legitimate radio stations – it was all about the pirates and waiting for my MCs to come on. It was proper, it was so big at the time. Every night I had it all planned out: I'm going to listen to Pay As

You Go 6.00 a.m to 8.00 a.m – it was all in two-hour slots – then So Solid, then Nasty Crew and so on. I was fanatical. I used to love it. I lived for it.

My favourite MC was called God's Gift, from Pay As You Go. I was also massively into Romeo, Mega Man, Asher D and Wylie. But God's Gift was my favourite; he was who I wanted to be. You'd got your rockers at school but for me it was all about a mike and two decks and the crews on pirate radio. If someone played me pop music, I'd think, 'Yeah, whatever, where's So Solid?' Quite stuck up in a way, but that was just what I wanted to do for a living, so that was what I listened to.

I worked hard at it too. I had things down to a T and monitored each line, often thinking, 'It's going to be impossible for me to write like that. How can I think of things like that?' The answer was practise, practise, practise. I would be kicking myself saying this is rubbish, then suddenly you'd do one rap and people would sit up and take notice, and that's when you'd taken it to the next level … then the next … and so on.

I was starting to buy Nike trainers and different styles of jeans and a sweatshirt, gear like that. I was adopting the music and then the trousers got lower and my accent started to change a bit. People would be saying, 'You come from a posh family and you live in a massive mansion [no I don't!]; why do you talk like that?' I would just say, 'Because that's the influences on my life. I don't have to be from a ghetto to rap, to MC. That's just what I am into.'

The biggest single influence as a band was without a doubt So Solid Crew (their biggest hit, '21 Seconds', would eventually come out just as we were recording our first demo). I guess an element of that appeal was the roughness they had – not Tupac or gangsta exactly, but they somehow felt like an American group. We used to practise down the alleys and have a laugh, saying this is what we are going to be doing, but of course we never ever thought it would come about. So Solid were *the* influence. We just wanted to be like them.

At the same time, we have never made out we are the same as them. Most of them grew up very rough in bad estates. We didn't grow up like that; we are totally different. We grew up quite middle class with only a little bit of trouble. I think we are totally different personality-wise too; the influence on us was just So Solid's whole image, the big numbers and the music.

One problem for us was that we wouldn't have gone to see So Solid live, because of the crowd they brought in; we were only kids after all. So we didn't get to see live garage acts. We got our fix mostly at an under-eighteens' every Thursday called Atlantis, at Epping Forest Country Club. I loved it. There'd be five DJs and four MCs – that was my live garage and I loved it with a passion, honestly. I wanted to be on that stage MC-ing at that club.

the
roller
coaster
begins

3

So, myself and those four mates were doing all these parties and calling ourselves Blazin' Squad; there was this rival crew we knew quite well from Chingford, a ten-minute walk away, calling themselves the Incredible Crew, a terrible name! We were friendly rivals, so there was a little bit of tension but it rarely got out of hand. It was just stuff like, 'You copied those lyrics, you use a beat counter and he doesn't', that kind of thing. Even so, we were making tapes and listening to each other's tapes when one of our friends, who was on work experience, started to tell us about what he was doing. Little did we know what was going to happen next.

This friend, Andrew Towers, was doing work experience at Xplosive Studios in Walthamstow, run by Terry and Taps, otherwise known as T&T. He'd been talking to T&T about what we were doing and how good he thought we were. T&T basically said, 'Show me the money, they can do it.' The deal was that for £200 you got your demo recorded and mixed.

Now we were always making tapes, but not a demo. Tapes were what we lived for. The idea of doing a demo was not to send it to record companies; it was purely to listen to ourselves and play at parties.

So we thought about the £200. We were so young and that seemed like a lot of money. There were five and five of us, two crews, but we reckoned there's already groups of five; there's no groups of ten out there. That would only be £20 each. That's realistic. It's not realistic for a fifteen-year-old to get £40 overnight, but you can borrow £20. I tell you what: it's the best £20 I've ever borrowed. It really was.

So we got the money together and booked the studio time. Merging the two rival crews, we decided to stick with our name, Blazin' Squad. On the actual day of the recording session, I woke up very early, picked up my pieces of paper and practised like mad – I'd been up late the night before practising until I fell asleep too. We went in to record just the one song. The demo was completed over three or four visits during the course of about two weeks.

Terry & Taps walked into the studio so relaxed and said, 'Right, what can you do?' I didn't have a clue what to expect, but they came across like they were all right; they came across well. They were good to us; they had some mad ideas too. They got the beats together for the tune; I give it to 'em, they pulled their weight and a good beat out of the bag. We took it home, had a riot with lyrics and came back to record our vocals. There were nine MCs on the track, which was called 'Standard Flow'. I wrote a bit more than everyone else, mainly because I was always writing. I was known to write so much, everyone kinda respected it; that was just the way it was (I often write last thing at night when I go to bed).

So then it was time to record each one of us for the first time. When it was my turn, I just kind of stood there and started doing my thing with my head down. I'd never stepped into a studio before; it was dark and moody and I was really quite nervous. It was quite intimidating for a fifteen-year-old. I'd done all of this on a mike at parties before, but now I had to shut the booth, put the headphones on and speak into this really expensive mike … it was weird. Even not being able to hold the mike the way I normally would was unsettling. But we soon got into it and adapted pretty quickly. My lines went at the end of the song deliberately, because Romeo rapped last on So Solid's '21 Seconds'. He was a ladies' man but could still rap and hold it, and I thought, 'Yeah, that's what I wanna do.'

T&T did all the mixing so that when we went back a week later it was all done and sounding wicked. When we got there, they said, 'Do you want to come back and make some more tunes?' We explained we hadn't got any money and 'we've got this one song, we'll go', but they said, 'That's cool, we'll cover these extra tracks.' So we ended up with four tracks from those very first sessions: 'Standard Flow' (straight garage), 'Easy Come, Easy Go' (a club banger), 'Offering' (a love song) and 'Joe' (a deep story). I've got to be honest – I didn't even know why we were recording four songs, but they said they'd cover it … we were only fifteen, why wouldn't we, really?

But we still loved our parties! Only things were never going to be quite the same again. Before the next party,

our song had been played on Y2K, one of our favourite pirate radio stations growing up. We all taped the show and took it into school to let everyone listen to it. When the DJ played 'Standard Flow' and shouted out to us, that was a milestone. Another big moment was when we played the demo at a party for the first time; it was just really special, a good moment for us. It kind of felt like the birth of everything (it is well known that EZ and Dreem Team were also playing it a lot – at that point it was on our own Weighty Plates label). That studio date, that one song … it just kicked everything off for us. Pretty soon, however, getting played on pirate radio was going to be overshadowed big time.

Sadly, we don't really see eye to eye with T&T now, but I've got a lot to thank them for, 'cos at the end of the day they rang George Tykeiff at East West Records, played him our demo and said, 'Come and

kenzie

We were offered a record deal less than a month after George heard the demo

meet these boys!' At the time we heard this we all hoped he might like it; we later found out he said he would sign us after hearing only thirty seconds of 'Standard Flow'.

I remember leaving a geography lesson to go to meet the 'A&R of Warner', which meant absolutely nothing to me as a fifteen-year-old. Me, Plat-Num and Reepa had these notes from our parents and all our mates were like, 'What you doing bunkin' off? They ain't real notes!' We just said, 'Trust us!'

We went to Xplosive to meet George, which shows how keen he was – an A&R man coming to the East End! He met all ten of us and loved us, and we felt he could see the way forward for us. So that was that. We'd only made the tape to play at parties, see how it went down with our mates. We were offered a record deal less than a month after George heard the demo. A £400,000 advance over a five-album deal. We didn't even have management at that point, just a lawyer, Alexis Grower, to help us. We were

mostly fifteen and all still at school. Crazy! I just couldn't believe it.

We signed the record contract at Sticky Fingers restaurant, which was nice. I had a few glasses of champagne and was sick out the back. The next day, we were due back at school and everyone was crowding round, saying, 'Where were you yesterday, then?' We told them we'd been signing a record deal and they were all like, 'Yeah, right!'

The only thing we were missing was a manager. Our lawyer, Alexis, said he could recommend someone who was used to dealing with big groups. His name was Albert Samuel. We asked Alexis who he looked after. 'So Solid.' Oh my God! We couldn't believe it. Albert's been wicked, very supportive. He always tells us straight, pure blunt: 'Was that good, Albert?' 'No, you can do much better.' You got to love that! We felt like we had to go with who knows best and that was Albert. He often says he believes in us more than we do ourselves and that has been a great thing to know. He's become a mate, too, over the years. I can phone him about other things that are nothing to do with music. With girls and stuff like that I will ring him and ask his advice and he will always talk to me. He is a top man and he's been good to me. When it was quiet for us later in our career, he slapped a contract on the table and said, 'I want to take you on for another three years. I believe in you boys.' He is quality and he has to be given respect for how he has looked after us.

I look back now and think there are a few reasons why we were signed so quickly by a major record label, when all we'd wanted was to press up a tune to play at parties. There were ten boys, and we looked totally different. They obviously thought we could appeal to the girls and, without sounding flash, I think there were ten quite good-looking boys there. Plus, the Squad has got a lot of mixes in there: one of us is from Barbados, one is mixed race, I'm obviously half-Asian/Indian, another one's Asian, one's Turkish, one's Greek and some are white; it's an amazing mix. That was undoubtedly part of it.

The track helped, of course. If I am being honest, I would say it was half-music, half-image. Then there was what was happening with garage at the time. So Solid had entered the charts at Number 1 the week we finished our demo. Before that they'd had success with 'Oh No' and an underground hit with 'Dilemma'. Then here we were, a younger, smaller crew, with a wicked tune and a good image, so it slotted in very naturally. So Solid's commercial success definitely helped us – which was fitting really as they were the single biggest influence on us in the first place, as I've said. We've obviously got to meet them on many occasions since we share a manager, and they've been really cool with us. I occasionally meet up for a bit of lunch with Harvey (he's one of the more sociable ones); Romeo's cool, Mega was cool when we spoke to him, Neutrino is just quality – we went out on a night with him and got smashed and got a few girls. I haven't met all of them. Some of them look a bit unapproachable but at the same time I can understand that; that's probably how they grew up, to be alert and not really let anyone in. The majority of them are cool.

Next thing we know, the record company want to fly us to Cape Town, South Africa, to film a video! We went into school and told all our mates and they were like, 'What?!' We needed the old notes from the parents again. By this time it was blowing up for us, proper involved.

kenzie

We flew out to Cape Town and the director actually got pneumonia so we ended up with a free holiday while new arrangements were made. The video itself was incredible; it must have cost hundreds of thousands of pounds. There was a mad go-karting scene, a broken-down freeway where they shut off the traffic for us, helicopters flying overhead, all sorts of stuff. It was amazing. Absolute madness. I didn't know what was going on, but I was loving it. We weren't thinking, 'Yeah, we are pop stars!'; we were just thinking, 'We are on holiday, making music, doing what we love but in a hot place. What a touch!' That was our attitude for a long time.

I enjoyed being in front of a camera for the first time, although I didn't know what I was doing. The weird thing was, the video in Cape Town got scrapped! Also, 'Standard Flow' was never fully released and didn't even make the first album. Why? Well, it was all changing with the garage scene and this had a big impact on what we were doing.

In between times, garage had been getting its fair share of bad press; there had been some shootings, most famously at a So Solid show at London's Astoria. Suddenly the media were all over the scene, talking about the violence and really bad-mouthing it. Now the prospect of a young, teen garage act suddenly wasn't so appealing to the record company perhaps. What I do know happened was that our music was taken in a much more pop vein. We were being called 'the junior So Solids' in some places, something certain people thought we had to get away from.

'Standard Flow' had reached Number 3 in the garage charts and we'd even got some good shout-outs in the garage underground press, such as Rewind. We were getting tunes played on pirate radio and there was a little hype about us, a bit of bubble on the streets. We did a remix with Elephant Man and that tune was big on the scene; we got Ras Kwame to mix it and it was a massive garage tune. They play it to this day. I'll flick on the radio and they still play Blazin' and Elephant Man. However, as soon as it became apparent that we would be doing pop, that all stopped overnight. Finished. The price we had to pay for going down the pop route was credibility on the street. That went straight out the window; they'll pick you up and drop you back down. That's when the boys started hating; the girls were loving us but the boys were hating us.

We had a meeting at Strider's with our manager, Albert, and he explained that he felt the garage angle was, for us at least, going nowhere. The track 'Crossroads' – a classic tune written by Bone Thugs-N-Harmony as a tribute to Eazy-E – was put forward as our first single. When that was suggested, you could hear the room go 'Oooooh'. It was one of the biggest selling singles ever in America; it hit Number 8 in the UK. It was a classic tune and some of us were not sure how a cover by Blazin' Squad would be received. But in the end we decided we were bringing that dedication to England, and that's more respect for Eazy-E; plus we are all big fans of NWA so for us to get to cover his dedication song felt like an achievement.

We recorded the cover and did a video for it at Canary Wharf. They used some footage of Cape Town as well. This new video was a lot cheaper, using those old clips and paying for ten cabs out of the East End! Do you know what I mean?

I remember very clearly our first ever gig. It was for an under-eighteen night in a club called Amadeus in Rochester, Kent. I wore a biker jacket and a pair of white jeans, so I was not looking good at all! We were nervous but it was very good, loads of screaming and stuff. It was so very different from what we were used to, though. In a party you are doing your thing, people are dancing and there are mates all around you, but on stage everyone is looking straight at you. For some reason, I've always felt quite vulnerable on stage – anyone could throw stuff. I've been punched in the jaw, someone threw ice in my face in Ireland, we were once hit with a few eggs at a Christmas lights event – but what can you do? Fortunately we only usually get ladies' knickers or bras. Although I once got a wedding veil with a girl's phone number on it!

Suddenly, aged fifteen and sixteen, we were about to face the press. Albert was one step ahead of the game and had us what is known as 'media-trained'. It might sound a bit fake but it was actually very useful. It took place with Andi Peters, the former presenter and producer, and he schooled us in various aspects of dealing with the press,

TV, cameras, interviews and stuff like that. Don't chew gum on telly; make eye contact with your interviewer – all that kind of thing. I think at such a young age we needed some tips, otherwise it could have been like throwing us to the lions.

I remember one of the very first radio shows we did was Simon 'Schoolboy' Phillips on Capital Radio. That was one of the main early interviews that stands out for me because of the amount of positive energy he showed us. He is quite urban himself and he took us on and was really good to us: 'my boys are in the studio!' He really made us feel welcome. Funnily enough, the very first magazine article we did was in *The Face!* They were really into us and it's funny to look back on that now because, pretty soon after, they wouldn't touch us with a barge pole!

Of course, the teen mags went mad for us. Every single one of them wanted us on the cover – *Smash Hits, Sneak, Top of the Pops,* all of them. We loved all that. Who wouldn't? It wasn't the magazine articles that made me think I was in a band and out there, though – I remember looking on the internet at an online record shop waiting for my song 'Crossroads' to come up in the search engine. When it did, I couldn't believe my eyes!

Suddenly, aged fifteen and sixteen,
we were about to
face the press

To promote the release of our debut single, 'Crossroads', we toured loads of schools over an intense two-week period. I loved these shows, I really did. We used to get up early, go to the school, perform, have a little chat with the crowd, answer a few questions, then me, Plat-Num and Flava would MC, so we'd still have that garage thing in there. Flava would beatbox, then we'd get someone else up from the school to MC against me. It was a really good laugh.

The best school show of the lot was when we went back to Highams Park, our own school, the one we had only just left! Imagine that! I was talking to various teachers about the band, thinking, 'Yeah, you slung me out of class a year ago and now you want my autograph for your daughter? Yeah, sure!' That's enough pleasure for me right there, on its own. There were Arsenal boys giving it the big 'un, and I MC-ed against one in particular and finally got to embarrass him, which was nice.

At the same time, we were still a garage crew at heart, so looking at the young ages of all these kids was a bit puzzling at first. Then I just thought, 'Let's be grateful for what we've got, a record deal. This could give us opportunities to go back and do your garage in the future.' However, now I am pleased that we didn't do garage 'cos it would have done nothing for our lives; it wasn't the way forward. Besides, that's something I will never complain about. I am grateful for all the fans I've got, regardless of their ages.

The way the hype blew up around us was just incredible. We were going to roadshows alongside big acts and getting the biggest reaction, even though no one really knew who we were. Mind you, I'm not so sure about what we were wearing! Man! We wore ten Adidas tracksuits, three in blue, four in green, four in red. It looked terrible!

Out on the road you quickly learn, though. One time Liberty X were on stage and we wanted to check them out so we walked up to the stands to watch. Then, as we sat down, the whole crowd spotted us and turned to scream and wave at us, even though Liberty X were still performing. That was disrespectful on our part to that band. We didn't mean it, of course, and I think they knew we were new to it all, but it was a lesson learnt.

The only thing I didn't like about that period was the story we told the media about how we came to release 'Crossroads'. We said at the time that our DJ had flicked on MTV and heard the song and that was that. Not true. The song was brought to us as a single. We didn't pick it ourselves. So it felt uncomfortable repeating that to magazines, but I can see why people advised us to do that.

Besides, what was about to happen with the debut single justified it all ...

top
tens and
four tales

Our schedule right at the very start was just unbelievable. We did our exams and left school in May, already with a record deal signed. We recorded **Crossroads**, did the school tour, loads of PAs (personal appearances) and promotion in June and July, and the single was released in August, the same week we received our GCSE results. We'd done all this crazy promotion but at the end of the day it all came down to whether anyone would actually buy the single.

On the Wednesday of release, the management phoned us with our mid-week chart position: Number 1.

'But don't get your hopes up yet because there's a Dr Dre song at Number 2 coming up strong behind you …'

I couldn't quite believe my ears.

'Hold on a sec, what did you just say? Dr Dre? Catching *us*? All right, cool … just give me a few moments to breathe!'

My exam results came that week but I was like, 'Yeah, *whatever*, what chart position are we gonna get?'

It was so unreal. By the Saturday, we were all nervous. I'd have been happy with a Number 2 – of course I would – but knowing you might be at Number 1, you really want it. I was really worried, thinking, 'Oh no! Everyone's going to go out today and buy the Dre song!'

They didn't. More than 52,000 people bought our tune.

'Crossroads' entered the charts at Number I.

When they told us the news, we went out into an alleyway outside Xplosive Studios and were popping bottles of champagne, dancing about, shouting, screaming, cheering. It must have made a strange sight at midday on a Sunday.

We didn't care. We were Number 1.

We recorded our debut album, *In The Beginning*, in Chiswick with Cut Father and Joe. The production on that record is spot on, especially for your average pop album. One of my favourite experiences from those sessions was going to Ireland to work with Biff (Richard Stannard) and Jules. We were put up in a nice hotel, the studio was massive and we were working with these two producer/songwriters who'd worked with the likes of the Spice Girls, Westlife, Five and Kylie. Their walls were covered in platinum discs and it was so exciting. Interestingly, given the more pop sound that most of the album was taking, they wanted to lead us down a more urban route, so the whole episode was very enjoyable.

Unlike at that very first demo, in the studio I felt much more chilled out; I was getting more confident on the mike and in the booth. That first time I'd put on a pair of headphones and rapped into a mike at Xplosive, it was

kenzie

like, 'This ain't how I used to do it,' but by the time we were doing the album I knew this was how everyone did it and I adapted. Spitting into a ten-grand mike is different from shouting out to your mates at a party, but when you sign a record deal that's the sort of change that you have to get used to very quickly.

Personally, I wasn't into a few songs on the debut album. I hated 'Love On The Line' with a passion. We didn't write it; we didn't even write the raps. I just thought it was 'Another Level/Freak Me', and I was convinced this was not what we should be doing. That was pencilled in as a single and we recorded the video on some really rough estate; people were throwing hard-boiled eggs out the windows at us and someone even soaked a *Yellow Pages* in water and threw it from the top of a council tower block. We had to get so many police down there. It was so unnecessary. That was our second single and most of us weren't happy. I certainly wasn't, but I listened to what they had to say. Nonetheless, the song charted at Number 6, so we had got another Top Ten under our belt.

kenzie

Our third single was a double A side of 'Reminisce/ Where The Story Ends', but almost all the airplay and promotion was around 'Reminisce'. I thought the flip was one of the best songs we'd ever written; it was done with Biff and it was just wicked. Also, Plat-Num, Flava and myself wrote the chorus so we were really proud of that tune. And we did our best ever video for it – all studio and live shots, behind-the-scenes if you like, and everybody loved it. That single hit Number 8. Only what seemed like a few months earlier we had been at school, revising for exams (supposedly!) and now we had three Top Ten hits!

The album sold very well and reached Number 24. The press coverage was strong, too. Although the garage press had disowned us for taking the pop route, we did get some surprising shouts from magazines like *NME*, who gave the album 3/5. There was barely time to pause for breath as we headed out on a promotional tour to plug the record. The pace of our life was staggering.

One story that really sticks in my mind from those early days was our debut *Top of the Pops* performance with 'Crossroads'. That was a big enough experience on its own, of course, but while we were there Robbie Williams came over to us and said, 'All right, guys, you lot are quality, keep doing your thing. I bigged you up on the radio the other day!' We were just standing there, open-mouthed, trying to be cool, but actually thinking, 'Who? Us?' Then we watched him do his recorded performance and it was amazing. To see that confidence … he didn't care, he was swinging the mike round, dancing, laughing, and I thought to myself, 'That's what I am gonna be like …' We were only seventeen at the time and that had a big impact on us all. I am sure Robbie probably didn't even notice but that was a key experience, for me at least.

We had chaperones when we first started out on tour. Mums and dads came on the road because we were so young – my dad came to quite a few gigs with us. It was a bit … not embarrassing … but imagine, you are turning up to a gig with all these pop stars and you've got chaperones – your parents! – looking over you. Don't get me wrong; none of us are ashamed of our parents, far from it, but it's just you are in your zone and you want to do your own thing. Besides, how am I going to chat to one of Girls Aloud when one of my best mate's mum is over the other side of the room?

The fans on tour are just incredible (the so-called Blazers). Our first tour was called 'In the Beginning'.

kenzie

was actually quite shy on those debut dates, so when it came to girls I didn't do much. That first series of shows was absolutely mental. We did twenty-seven dates, including two Manchester Apollos, two Hammersmiths; it really was the time of my life. Our merchandise couldn't be printed up quick enough to meet demand!

Sometimes with the ten of us out there things can get a little out of hand on tour. We are actually banned from the Malmaison chain of hotels 'cos a window 'fell out'. I think a telly fell out too. Plus, we had to refund twelve guests, rooms were trashed and they got really annoyed with us … which is fair enough, I suppose.

Vince Langdon and Phil Byrne took us on that first-ever tour and they weren't best pleased. Our security man was called Ian – we call him Blonx (slang for massive) – and he was there having to look after all of this chaos, running around after ten of us. It wasn't always us who caused the problems. On one occasion we were all in the tour bus when they shouted, 'GET DOWN ON THE FLOOR! NOW!', and bricks came smashing through the windows! Their's is not an easy job, I am telling you.

My security man, Ian Norrington, has seen some funny goings-on during his time with us on the road.

When some New Age travellers brought crates of eggs to throw at us in Sheffield, Ian just piled in there and destroyed the lot! Another time we were shooting a video in a cold, dank lido that was supposed to be all sunny – they put so many strong lights on to create the summery effect that most of us got our skin burnt! Then some haters started throwing rocks over the wall so Ian stormed off, perched on top of this six-foot wall trying to catch hold of these people. It wasn't all bad though – on my very first tour date ever, I wasn't yet sharing with Ollie; instead it was Ian! After the show, we got back to the hotel room and there were all these notes from girls asking after me, which I think was quite funny for Ian to see!

Not wanting to give the game away, but on the road we all used to check in under false names, like most pop stars. I was Mosh and Ollie was Ino; Tom and Stuart were Porn and Star; Rocky and Melo were Knee and Gro; Sam and Flava were Ee and Jat; Lee and Mus were

Little and Heads. It didn't really make much difference because girls would get the room number anyway … somehow they always seemed to find us out!

The fans of Blazin' Squad are just unreal. I've jumped into the crowd before and then been proper dragged down into the pit, my shirt ripped off, rings taken off me, my trainers pulled off. The grip these girls have is amazing! Sometimes you want to push them away but then you remember they are only young.

I had a tendency to wander off from security, especially early on, but I have learnt my lesson. One time I walked off I was rushed by about forty girls and, I've got to be honest, it was pretty scary. They were mad! Also, when we leave a venue, it is always worrying that one of them might fall under the wheels of the bus – they are so excited and running after us, it's a real fear.

We do sometimes argue but only ever about stupid things, such as who is the best rapper: Flav thinks Jay-Z, Ollie thinks Eminem and we will proper get into it. It's natural when there are ten boys out on the road under such demanding circumstances. I like it; I'd be annoyed if we didn't argue at all. I wouldn't even call it arguing; it's usually more a debate. Minimal arguments, minimal.

kenzie

kenzie

We've played Wembley Arena about four times as shows and sold it out on our own tour once. That's 11,000 people! What a buzz that headline slot was! That night is easily the highlight of our live career for me so far (although playing Party In The Park and meeting Prince Charles was wicked too). For some reason, I decided to wear a parka jacket, and with thousands of people crammed in there it was like a sauna already, so I had one sweaty night! I had to have a few beers before we went on stage – I remember on our rider we had chewing gum, Haribos, champagne, Stella and condoms. Gotta be done, innit! It was so nerve-wracking, I kept thinking back to the first time on tour at Bristol Colston Hall which was in front of 1,000 people. Now

We played 'Bounce' and we'd come out individually – I was fourth. It was truly unbelievable, quality. The nerves quickly turned to adrenalin and that takes you through, no matter how exhausted you feel. We weren't just on playback, like on some previous dates: we had a live band, so the vibe was amazing, there were fireworks going off everywhere, deafening screams, hundreds of banners, everyone was going absolutely ballistic! …

and I was thinking, 'This is where I wanna be!' For me to sign a deal at sixteen and then to find myself playing Wembley at eighteen – I just thought, 'This can't be real!'

Introducing
the squad

5

He's kind of known as the ginger one! He's the one I got into it all with, who I started MC-ing with. He lives about fifty yards away, so I am always round there. Our parents get on well too, which helps, and I get on really well with his family. He was one of my best friends from day one. I've got a really good relationship with his dad, John; if I ring his house and Flava's not in, I talk to his dad. Flava is the music boy; he comes from a really musical family and is probably the most musically talented of us.

James Murray
aka Flava

He can play piano, he used to play trumpet and guitar, he's got his own studio, and I am sure that on production he will go very far – he's already producing very alternative soundtracks for films. Generally, I rely on him a lot, I can talk to him for hours; we've got a good trust going on. He is very laid back, I haven't seen him lose his temper for years and it will take a lot to push him – whereas I am the complete opposite! People like management liaise with him first – he kind of adopted that role – which is fine. I wouldn't say he is the leader, but he has been involved in it all probably the longest.

He is absolutely mad with a few drinks inside of him! He's changed a lot recently, though. We used to wear a lot of hip-hop gear but now we are changing that and looking a bit more mature. Flava gave all his tracksuits to charity and is dressing really well now. We've had to grow up quite fast and maybe our appearance has been pulling us back down sometimes. Our record company and management used to say, 'Can't you change the clothes? You know, don't wear tracksuits?', but we wouldn't have it. I kinda regret it in a way, but we were young and we just wanted to do our own thing.

I met Chris at the same time as Flava, sitting on that same park bench. Me and Flava had already started MC-ing, so we invited Chris round. When we asked him, he said, 'Yeah, I've been writing some stuff as well!' We took him round the corner to this place we used to call The Arsehole (we had The Arsehole, The Block, Brookfield and The Shithole: we used to hang around all the top places!). It took us a while to get him to MC and when he did we were like 'Woah!' I was never expecting him to be that good. At first he just used to sit in and listen, watching and learning and not taking part too much, but slowly he got his confidence up. When we later recorded our first ever demo, he was the one who kicked off the track – he was going to America and wanted to get on the song, so he went out of his way a week before to go in there, which makes him the first person ever to rap on a Blazin' Squad track.

Me and him make a really good double team. We'll be at each other's throats one night, drunk, then the next minute we are joking; we really work together well, feed off each other. He is an MC and rapper and one of the main vocal men. He's a great dancer too.

Chris McKeckney aka Melo-D

Sam Foulkes aka Spike-E

If I remember rightly, he could well have been on that famous park bench as well! He says I taught him to MC but I didn't; he just came around and watched, like Melo-D, and got into it. I'd say he is probably one of the best now, arguably the top lyricist of the three of us. So he's come a long way since copying Neutrino! We get on really well, and he never takes things too seriously. He used to row with the record company and was more forward, saying stuff which perhaps didn't do him any favours, but at the same time he always got his point across and I respect him for that. He rings me every day, often just to make sure I am all right. Sometimes I have to switch off from the world, so it's hard to get through to me, but he will call me every day. He is loyal to me and really proud of what I did in the *Big Brother* house.

I met Ollie in Oakhill. We used to go round and sit in his loft and smoke, play music, do our thing. He was a wicked footballer: he got into it the same time as Melo-D and Spike-E. He is really sociable and polite even though he's been through some quite tough life experiences. He's a strong boy and for that I look up to him. He's the only one of the band who has his own flat, so it's going really well for him. We met through football and to this day he really winds me up, mucking about all the time: 'You got a new girlfriend? When you getting married?' In return I'll say stuff like, 'Warm my shower up for me. Do you know who I am?'

He is my room-partner on tour, so we know each other very well. He will always leave me the room if I have pulled; he's always willing to go and sleep on someone else's floor (and vice versa). The rules of the tour! He's been my room-partner for three years so we have our routines – I will lie in 'til the last possible second while he is in the shower almost ready! If I didn't have him, I would probably still be in bed at a hotel from last year. He sorts things out for me; he's always running round for me and looking after me when we are away.

He's another one who voices his opinion strongly to the record company and he gets very involved, which is good; you need people like that. He's got a bit of a temper as well; he rises to a bit of hate but it is hard not to sometimes. At the end of each night we will analyse the gig in the hotel room, but we talk a lot about ex-girlfriends too, especially if we've had a few drinks – we both had long relationships when we were younger. He is a confident talker on TV, he does a lot of rapping in the band and does his best to get involved in songwriting. We are tight.

These four – Flava, Melo-D, Spike-E, Freek – and myself made up the original Blazin' Squad.

kenzie

Ollie Georgiou aka Freek

Of the rest of Blazin' Squad, I'll start off with Reepa, the first of the Chingford crew who, as I've said, were known as the Incredible Crew before we merged. I've known him since we were in nursery. I actually think Reepa was in the same maternity ward as Flava so they go back even further than that! We've been best mates for years now. When I came out of the *Big Brother* house, he said, 'I thought I'd lost my best mate to that Jeremy!' No way.

We can get a bit cheeky with girls; we often go out with sisters or cousins. We haven't done twins yet. We have a fierce rivalry over that; there's always a bottle of champagne at the end of the year. Having said that, in 2005 it's £500 and two bottles of champagne, because I feel quite confident! Reepa is more into rock and pop; he likes Blue. He wants to make a million pounds and try to make it as a hip-hop star.

I've known him since our footballing days. He was a very talented footballer and could have gone far in the game, but when we were still young he broke his leg very badly in a game on the pitch next to me. I remember it well; he never really recovered from the injury and that was a great shame. That injury and what happened after really hit him hard.

One thing you notice about Strider is that he is always writing lyrics all the time; his book is always packed. His dedication to that is immense. He is also one of the vocal boys. He was the one I'd do a lot of the front covers with: the pin-up men! He was a lot more popular than me, though, at signings and all that; he used to get loads of teddies and presents constantly. We would both do well, but he was the popular one. If you meet him in the flesh, he looks exactly as he does on TV. Whereas if you meet me, my hair probably ain't gelled, my skin's quite bad and all that. Strider always looks fresh and proper, looks after himself.

kenzie

Mus Omer aka **Strider**

Marcell Somerville aka Plat-Num
formerly known as Rocky B

I didn't really know him that well at the start of school. He was massive in school, always towering over people. We'd have geography lessons together with him and Reepa but then, when we began to talk about So Solid, we quickly bonded and could always chat about that underground music vibe. He had his own crew back then and was known as an MC. From the Chingford lot he was one of the first, like myself in Highams Park, but neither of us knew that for a while. Then he said, 'Shall we come over and make a few tapes together?' When he did, he was proper on top of his game and everyone was well impressed. We'll have him in!

He's mad as anything now; he has these half-hour mad stages, all hyperactive. It's hilarious. He'll come up to me and just slap me in the face and I'll be like 'What?!' It's good fun, though; I've rarely seen him angry. Someone once threw Coke on his Avirex jacket in Romford and he went absolutely mad.

A lot of boys look up to him as the ideal hip-hop boy; his look suits the hip-hop wear proper. He loves his gangsta pimpin' thing, decorating his room after *Scarface*! He can pull it off. The boy fans go to him; they take him more seriously. The crowd love him and he loves the crowd.

In the studio he's always got mad ideas and is probably the most creative one of the lot. He's so creative 24/7, making beats, writing songs; he has a real ear for music. When I split up with a girlfriend in 2004, we were on our way to a gig in Ireland and everyone was hyped up except me. Plat-Num saw I wasn't happy and came and sat at the back of the bus with me and we just talked the whole way. You need people like that around you.

Krazy left Blazin' Squad a short while after I came out of the *Big Brother* house, but I still love him to bits! It was a shock, a bit weird, but I wish him the best of luck. He's generally quite quiet but he has his mad phases as well, especially if he's had a drink. I don't think I've ever had an argument with him in my life. He's proper into his fitness – he runs mini marathons and all that. He came out of his shell on 'Flip Reverse', which was really all about him; he was the hype and the front man. He looked good. I was still in an Avirex but he'd stepped up a level; he looked like a proper pop star, getting older fans. He was in his element.

kenzie

Lee Bailey aka Krazy

Tom Beasley aka Tommy B

He's the DJ. I've known him since the start of school.
We were two DJs from separate crews when we first met,
so there was always going to be that friendly rivalry.
He really shone back then; he loves his music and knows
it inside out. He is proper up to date on stuff too –
fashion, music, everything. He goes out and DJs at clubs
on his own and is really stepping into his zone. He's one
of the cleverest of the squad too: nine GCSEs, all top
grades. Bright boy. He's quite quiet, but very sarcastic
and cocky, like me. He's got a lot going for him.

introducing the squad

We always say we are going to take our time with the next record but our schedules are so mad it never happens. Before we started work on the second album we said we would write and record forty songs, then whittle it down to a dozen or so for the final selection. No chance!

We recorded *Now Or Never*, our second album, at some real proper studios, such as Townhouse and Metropolis in London. I really enjoyed working in those sorts of places. I actually came up with the name for that record, which I am proud of.

We were much more involved in the second album. Flava produced a song on it, we all got into it and the vibe was really good. It was great to be working with people like Dennis Ingoldsby, Chris Ballad and Andy Murray, as well as top songwriters like Obie and Jane Vaughan (they came up with the hook for 'Flip Reverse'). One of my favourite tracks was a ballad called 'Missing You', which was a killer tune. I wish we'd put that out as a single. They went with 'Flip Reverse' and that got us our biggest hit since 'Crossroads', at Number 2. Result! We toured that record heavily too and it did well, selling a similar amount to the debut.

We had some great times on the road promoting that album too. We did these mini seaside tours and one time we all went to the beach and got our rubber dinghies out. Flava was in a dinghy with Freek and they were a good thirty feet out from the shore. Our tour manager at the time, Vince, picked up a crab and threw it and it smacked Flava bang on the side of his

head. Flava thought someone had thrown a brick; Freek panicked and banged Flava on the other side of his head with the oar and they both fell out of the dinghy!

Probably the hardest part of being in Blazin' Squad is the misconception people have about us that we are wannabe gangstas. The press have picked up on it and we've had our fair share of negative coverage (although when *Loaded* called us Pokémon I laughed for days). That misconception does my head in. Hopefully, me going in the *Big Brother* house has brought across everyone's image in the band, not just mine. Now they know what we are really like – not this ridiculous wannabe image we've been credited with.

I know some of our videos might look that way and sometimes our clothes have given that impression – you know, the baggy tracksuits and the bling – but that's just not who we are or what we are about.

Our style has changed a lot since we started out. At first it was all tracksuit bottoms, jumpers, a few woolly hats. That's how we looked when we went to see George Tykeiff at East West Records that very first time. For the 'Crossroads' video they put us in the worst shirts of all time; even though they cost about £140 each they looked awful. It took us about two years to live that down! We smartened up for 'Love On The Line': I was in a Versace top and a parka coat. People started calling us chavs: we were even voted Number 8 in the 'Celebrity Chavs of the Year' chart! It went from that slowly but surely to the hip-hop clothing – but that generated a lot of bad feeling towards us. People don't like it when you turn up to a club in an Avirex, baggy jeans and Tims; they think, 'who are you trying to kid?' That look has got that stereotyped image, 50 Cent, this is for rappers and bad boys vibe. I just felt comfortable and liked it, though.

Every so often the record company and management have said to get stylists in but we've never had any of that. We've been really stubborn on that point, perhaps to our cost in the past, but you have to feel comfortable in what you are wearing. Now we are all wearing much smarter stuff; a few of the boys are even wearing suits when they go out and we all look a lot more mature.

Mind you, people might not say we were more mature if they knew about our video with a lesbian scene! It was the band's idea – for 'Here For One', our sixth single – and these two girls were really going for it, but it got cut. I thought it would be a quality publicity stunt; you never heard a room so quiet. I asked for an edit but they've never sent it to me!

The bad press has come alongside the haters too. We have had our fair share of haters. There are certain places I would never dream of going, certain areas, rough parts, certain clubs; they don't like what you are doing, they say you are not keeping it real or they are jealous of their girlfriends fancying you, or whatever. I think in our time we have been one of the most hated bands by boys and adults as well.

I changed my phone number six times in 2004. People ring you up and say, 'I know where you live, I'm gonna come and find you, don't walk out your house, make sure you are never seen in this area …' and so on. At first it was really quite scary but after a while you get used to it, and now I just think, 'How bored are you?' One thing we've all learnt is to rise above the hate. As someone once told me, you gotta be rated to be hated.

kenzie

this is big brother...

I was sitting on the toilet when my mobile rang one day in December 2004. I paused for a moment then decided to answer it.

'Morning, Kenz, it's Amy. The **Big Brother** people have been in touch and were wondering if you'd consider going on? Oh, and by the way, don't tell anyone ...'

My life was about to get seriously crazy.

Sometimes I'd watched *Big Brother* with the boys on tour. I wasn't a huge fan, but occasionally I'd say, 'I'd win that!', being my usual cocky, sarcastic self, winding them up. Then I got that phone call. It turned out that both myself and Lee had been put forward and a secret meeting was quickly arranged at a London hotel.

We went with Albert Samuel and his brother, Dave; I was so excited. I don't think Lee was so sure about it at that time but I already had my heart set on it. It was a weird meeting, though. The two people from *Big Brother* were talking really quietly, and we had to move about this lounge three times because they were so paranoid there might be a media mole eavesdropping or something. I was talking a lot, really trying to come across well, making eye contact, chatting away, I just really wanted to get in there.

Then nothing.

Christmas came and went and still nothing. I was sleeping quite badly, thinking how this could completely change my life, but why the silence?

Then the phone rang again.

'Hey, Kenz, you still up for *Big Brother* then?'

'Fill me in!'

We'd got this 'letter of consent' through but even then management were saying, 'Don't get your hopes up, don't believe anything until contracts are signed.' But I had my heart set on it even more now! I rang the office every day, 'Have they signed yet?' I knew it would mean so much to my life at that moment. I don't know to this day why they chose me but I just feel lucky. I would have been devastated if I'd not got it, I don't mind saying.

I don't think Albert wanted me to do it at all; he was really unsure about it. I said, 'Trust me, I won't mug anyone off, I will prove myself.' He told me that once I was in there I wouldn't be able to phone him to get me out if I didn't like it and I said no problem. Then he just said, 'You know what then? Go for it!'

One of the very first things which happened was they called me in to do a 'profile'. I'd been with the boys in Butlins until four in the morning and had to get up at seven but for once I was out of the door on time. I got to the West End at eight in the morning, to this little bar called Jewel in Covent Garden. They asked me all these questions, mostly 'Are you comfortable signing loads of medical forms?' I was, like, 'Yeah, *whatever*, sign, sign, sign!'

Suddenly it was the day before I was due to go into the *Big Brother* house. They gave me a nice suite in a top hotel and I planned to have a meal with some friends and management. In the afternoon, they came and inspected my suitcase.

'You aren't allowed to wear any logos at all.'

'What?'

'No logos. Sorry.'

All my clothes had were Ecko, Academic Wear, logos all over them. They were all three sizes too big, American stuff.

They stripped everything out of my case!

'I'm gonna be walking round naked. Oh my God.' I literally didn't have a stitch left once they'd taken all the logo stuff away. Luckily, my new tour manager, Mark Sutton, was on hand, thank God. I rang him in a panic and explained what had happened and he said, 'Don't panic, I am in the area, I'm just going for a bite to eat with someone then I'll be there at five.' I was still panicking down the phone and, quietly, he was like, 'Shut up, I'll be there.'

Mark drove over to me – he was all suited and booted for a meeting with his accountant – and we raced off to the West End. I jumped out of the car at Oxford Circus and … I'd forgotten my wallet! I didn't even have to ask Mark; he just wopped out a wad of cash and said, 'Give it back to me whenever.'

I ran into Topman at Oxford Circus and started grabbing – shirts, belts, jeans, hats. It was the biggest shopping spree I'd ever been on and it was all over in half an hour. I did get recognized and people asked for autographs but I was like, 'I am so sorry, I am in a mad rush. I can't tell you why. I'd love to tell you but I can't.'

I really enjoyed that shopping spree, though. I bought these cool shirts saying things like, 'Save water, drink beer', and I thought they really reflected my cheekiness. I bought seven shirts for seventy quid and I was like, 'Yes!' Of course, the irony was that once I was in the house I spent most of the time in a dressing gown and Caprice's pyjama bottoms (what a touch!).

I made it back to the hotel for the evening meal but the nerves in me were starting to rise. I didn't sleep at all the night before; I didn't know what to do with myself to be honest. I was told not to talk to anyone; they took my phones off me and gave me a chaperone to make sure I did what I was told. Then I was driven from the hotel to the Moathouse Hotel near Elstree Studios, where they film. I had to spend the entire day there with my chaperone. He was cool but if there was a knock at the door, even for room service, he would jump up and answer it. Then some *Big Brother* people came to brief me, but didn't really tell me anything, especially not who else was going in.

The last thing I watched on telly was *Richard & Judy* at 5.00 that night. At the end of the show they were saying, 'Tonight we will find out the contestants of *Celebrity Big Brother*. But before we do, we've got Vanessa Feltz here ...' and Vanessa comes on and says, 'Turn back now, it will kill you, you will go mad.' I was sitting there and my heart was pumping out of my chest, I was thinking, 'Cheers, Vanessa. That's really done me the world of good!'

We got a call to head out so we left the Moathouse and drove past the *Big Brother* house, with all these flashing lights; it was amazing. Then I was escorted with my chaperone to this little white room where I had to wait for forty-five minutes. It was the worst wait of my life; this room was like something in a mental hospital. They gave me some disgusting plate of pasta but I couldn't eat anyway; I didn't know what to do with myself. I was thinking, 'What am I doing here?'

Finally, there was a knock on the door and I was taken out and down this long corridor then hustled straight into a blacked-out Voyager. The driver said, 'I'll play you some music to calm you down', and he put on Jay-Z! I was like, 'I thought you was gonna bust a bit of opera, mate!' Don't get me wrong: I love Jay-Z to bits but he isn't really going to calm me down! Anyway, we were driving around, I thought to somewhere else first, but then suddenly we stopped, the door was opened and there was this massive flash of hundreds of cameras and tons of screaming. I stepped out ... straight on to the red carpet outside the house, and I could see Davina just a little way ahead of me. It was so weird.

I walked past some of the public and the one person whose hand I went to shake gave me a thumbs down instead. I thought, 'Mate, I'd kill you if ...' Then I saw the Blazin' boys and management and I was desperate to

go over to them. Davina said, 'Happy Birthday', gave me a hug and we had a quick chat, then I walked up this ramp to where a big bouncer was waiting. I half thought, 'What? Is he gonna want some ID?'

He moved to one side and a door opened for me to walk through. That was really strange: it was just a white path from the outside world to the house, like walking to the end of your life, to heaven almost. When the door shut behind me, there was no sound at all. I stood by the door at the other end of this white corridor and it opened … I was in the *Big Brother* house!

I walked in and everyone was like, 'Hello … who is that?' A few people knew me. Jeremy knew me, which was cool, but to be honest, as I said hello to people I looked around and thought, 'Who's that?' as well! I knew Jeremy and Caprice. Everyone seemed a lot older than me.

Brigitte was the last one in after me. Then it all started …

As I mentioned, it was my birthday that day so it was nice to get off on a good, positive note. They got me a magnum of champagne and everyone was nice to me.

They only played two songs at the 'party' and one of those was 'Flip Reverse' (the other was by Outkast)! Still, it was a good night; I had a few glasses of red wine and started to get to know everyone …

THE HOUSEMATES
On Jeremy Edwards

We'd met before so we knew of each other, but once in the house we just clicked. He really did look out for me. The one day I was depressed he noticed and said,

'Come on, man, you are bigger than this.' He would say stuff like, 'This is our last ever Monday', to make you feel better and he came up with all the games: the chess with the bottle-top pieces carved with nails, caps thrown into a cup, carpet bowling, all of that; he was an inspiration in the house.

I don't think he let his guard down very much, though, and, to be fair, I don't blame him, especially having been with Rachel Stevens. He was never gonna slip up – he's too clever – so you'd see him walk away when we started playing spin the bottle. He was one of these people who doesn't read the papers, still goes on the underground to work, that sort of approach to the fame game, which is fair enough. I respect him for that.

He did talk about some stuff, though, like public school; he told me all about that. I didn't have a clue and I was interested. He also explained all about his acting jobs and auditions, which was cool. But when it came to his love life and girlfriends, he was very careful – he told me he had a girlfriend but he didn't want to mention her name.

We laughed all the time in the house. When Jackie Stallone was banging her way along the bedroom like a pinball, it was just side-splitting. What I remember most of all was turning over and seeing this woman stumbling along, then bang! I was crying my eyes out, I couldn't breathe for laughing. Apparently, it's been listed as one of the funniest moments on TV. I can tell you, being there was even funnier; I nearly fell out of my bed.

On Lisa I'Anson

When I came out and people told me she had come across really badly, all bossy and that, I was amazed. I thought, 'How can she possibly have?' When I first got in there, she hugged me and said, 'It's all good,' and proper looked after me. When we were making the shopping list, if I wanted something Lisa would always speak up for me. She did everything for me, cooked for me, helped me wash up and looked out for me all the time. She was interesting as well, because she seemed to know a lot about the programme. I got on really well with Lisa.

On Germaine Greer

Apparently she spoke very highly of me, which was nice. Talk about intelligent! I would find myself chatting with her and thinking how powerful you must be to be

able to lecture at Cambridge; it was just on a different level. There I was, this nineteen-year-old rapper, talking with this massively intelligent woman. It was amazing. And she was never snooty with me, never. She looked out for me as well, cooking and stuff, and I was quite gutted when she left. I think she'd had a very interesting past and I really wanted to find out more – if she'd stayed for a game of spin the bottle, it would have got very interesting I think! She was upset, though, by *Big Brother* and just thought she was being mugged off.

On Bez

Bez is a legend. We had a right laugh. We used to work out together and stay up late drinking some nights. I felt for him 'cos he loves his weed, but he was deprived and I thought he was really going to flip out. He was really worried what his kids were going to think of him, getting

really wound up about it, and I said, 'Think how proud they are gonna be!' I was pleased for him that he won. I think he had a little bit of trouble before he went in and I think winning did a lot for him.

I will definitely keep in touch with Bez; I have his number and have texted him to hook up. On the final night of *Big Brother*, Bez went out with my boys – I couldn't go because I had to see family. They all rolled in at about half-eight the next morning … I don't even want to know what went on!

On Caprice Bourret

She is quality. Gorgeous, oh my God. When I was giving her a massage, I was just thinking, 'My boys are gonna be so jealous!' Obviously I fancy her, do you know what I mean? I walked in and saw her and thought 'Yeah, there's an ambition!'

Seriously, though, if it was just me and her in the room, I would come up with any conversation. We really did get on well and had a lot of long talks and played all the games. I really admired her because she's not your average glamour girl; she's got her head screwed on and knows exactly what she's doing. Like Jeremy, she had that guard up; she said so herself when we went into the blue room. People might criticize that but she might have been burnt in the past. Who knows? She is genuinely a nice girl, good to talk to, good to have a laugh with. So what if she doesn't give too much away? Since we came out I've spoken to her a few times, just to say hello; she even gave her number to a photographer to give to me, which was a touch. Then she invited me to a party. Sweet!

On John McCririck

Mate! A legend. I heard how he was hated. On the third day he called me 'weak'. I would have hit him. I was well drunk, but you can't talk to me like that; no one can ever talk to me like that. 'Don't start patronizing me!' The funny thing was, I'd only learnt the word 'patronize' a few minutes earlier. Jeremy had said it and I asked him what it meant. Then John said that about me so I thought, 'Fuck it, I'll use that word on him!' It came across quite well, I think!

Afterwards, though, I went to the diary room and explained how I am not aggressive and that I didn't want to come across like that, but everybody has said to me that I was just sticking up for myself. Then he went on his three-day silent protest, during which the only thing he said was 'Sorry' to me. I could have said, 'No, man, you are an idiot', but I just said, 'Cool.'

I didn't like his opinions about women – all the women hated him in there. I just said to him, 'Look, John, me and you have got a lot of different views on life;

let's just talk on a certain level. I don't want to talk about your left wing and your right wing, I don't get involved in politics.' He was big-time offensive to Caprice and Brigitte – when Brig walked in the room and he said 'disgusting', she couldn't believe it. Then he said about Caprice selling 'her grubby little bras'. It was out of order.

Yet, John would make me a cup of tea in the morning and we would have a laugh. He came up to me before he left and said, 'You are a good kid, you can go far; but don't let all this hooligan and yob behaviour affect you, tone down your swearing and the alcohol, and stop saying, "Do you know what I mean".' I said, 'That's a bit hypocritical, isn't it?' and he said, 'Yeah, I know. I am not saying look up to me, I'm just saying you could go far, just tone down the swearing and stop saying, "Do you know what I mean".' I thought, 'I must have got through.' He does like me; he plays the baddie but he likes me.

Me and some of the boys went to Sandown Races a few weeks after leaving the house and John came up, hugged me and said, 'Here's my boy!' We had a great laugh, rapping live on Channel 4; he was dancing and he loved it! I got £5 out of my wallet to put on a horse and John just grabbed about another £45 and I lost it all on this horse he tipped. It failed miserably. I lost about £250 on the races! He entertained me thoroughly in the house, he was so funny. It was a great shame when he left.

On Jackie Stallone

Oh my God! Jackie. When she walked in, I just thought, 'Is that real? What is that?' Even when Brigitte said it was Sylvester's mother, I was still in shock. We went up to her like a load of grandkids and she said to me, 'You could be my grandson …,' and I thought, 'Great!'

I was showing her round the house and she was saying she'd expected to go to a medieval castle with eight of the most intelligent people in Britain and I was like, 'Well, sorry, you ain't. I do apologize.' She did not have a clue what she was involved with, not a clue. I showed her the shower and she said, 'But you can see through …' It was hopeless trying to explain, really.

She started reading my palm, which was weird – Sylvester Stallone's mum reading your palm. She was saying, 'This is your love line, you've had a lot of trauma …' and all this sort of stuff. Then she said, 'I can read your feet', and I thought, 'You could but you're not going to!'

She was used to servants, she lives in Malibu and is Sylvester Stallone's mum. That was the bottom line. Jackie didn't do herself any favours, though. I made her a cup of coffee and toast one morning – she is, after all, an old woman. She called me a 'little boy' and John went mad; he was wild. He said, 'His name is *Kenzie!*' She said to me, 'What's your name?' and I said, 'Little boy, apparently.' There was just too much for her mind to take in.

It was just bonkers.

I can honestly say I have never, ever, met anyone like her.

On Brigitte Nielsen

One of my favourites. She is huge, a real presence. She looked out for me as well, big time. If she was cooking dinner for the group, she would ask me what I wanted and make that. If I was toasting a bagel, she'd be like, 'I'll do it for you!' She proper looked out for me – she said I reminded her of her son. That was cool.

I really felt sorry for her when Jackie came in and she was forced into such an awkward situation. I thought it was bang out of order to bring Jackie in, just a cheap publicity stunt, terrible. I couldn't believe it. Brigitte was going to leave so I stayed up the whole night 'til seven in the morning persuading her not to. Then when she didn't leave anyway, I thought, 'I could have gone to bed!'

I was really pleased that she stayed to the end. I thought she'd win off the back of her ex-mother-in-law coming in. She is a good woman and she didn't need that. When I came out, my mates were all saying, 'We thought you were gonna pull Brigitte!,' and I was like, 'Mate! She would eat me up!' Much as I would like to, she would swallow me whole.

People have come up to me and said they were gutted I didn't win, but I'm not. I read the front pages saying I was the biggest favourite in history, 10-1 and all that. It doesn't matter; it really doesn't. I've got so much out of it anyway. If I'd have known that I'd come second before I went in, I'd have been well chuffed!

8

taken to task

My daily routine in the **Big Brother** house consisted of this: get up late, cup of tea, exercise (with our fitness instructor, Caprice, which seemed really to motivate me for some reason), breakfast, by which time it was already early afternoon. Then I'd hit the Jacuzzi, sauna, have a shower, do a task, then probably have another shower 'cos of the filth, hit the sauna again, have a bit of dinner and kick back for the rest of the night. That might sound like a nice day, but, let me tell you, it was so boring at times. It is nothing like how you imagine on TV; they make it look so entertaining and fun with the tasks and all that. You might tune in to watch the evening show and they say 'Day 12: Big Brother has set up an obstacle course for the housemates' and we are all there having a laugh, but what it should actually say is: 'Day 12: Big Brother took over four hours to set up an obstacle course for the housemates and while they were doing it they locked everyone in the bedroom without anything to do, leaving them to all go stir crazy.'

The last few days were the hardest, when there was hardly anyone to talk to. It was depressing, and it did get me down. By Day 16 I was getting really down and briefly thought about leaving. But then I said to myself, I've only got two more days, I don't want to be weak. I was so bored, though; I missed my family, my boys, my music, everything. It was hard being without music. I listen to music every single day; it is my motivation.

There are so many elements of *Big Brother* that are much harder than you expect. One of the most difficult aspects for me was the age gap. I was the only teenager and everyone else was in their thirties or older. I was convinced they'd put a young girl in there with me, not to pull but just to be on the same wavelength. When I walked in and saw the age of the group, I was really intimidated and just thought, 'How can you do that to me? How am I gonna get my point across? Are they gonna take me seriously?' Then I just thought, 'Hold on a minute! I am going for it! I am an east London boy and I can mouth off back!'

Despite the age gap, another big surprise was how well I got on with everyone. People were interested in what I had to say and what I did. It was hard for me to get involved in the politics – I don't know anything about that – but it didn't seem to matter. It was also surprising the way everyone looked out for me.

Big Brother was evil too. Dropping breakfast on my head, the Brigitte/Jackie thing, making us walk through pigs' blood and compost, plucking pheasants – oh my God! When I saw my pheasant, I thought, 'I will be hard here and rip the wing off', but its head fell off! Germaine had done it before so she helped me, which was a result!

The best task was the song that me, Brigitte and Bez did; that was quality. The worst one was when we had to spin on the merry-go-round then trawl through the pigs' blood, the compost, the eggs, the cigarette butts and all that. I'd said to myself, I won't be sick on TV: first task I was sick four times. It wasn't about the blood and compost and all that; it was being on the merry-go-round for ten minutes. Disgusting! Speaking of which, I blocked the toilet about five times, but I blamed everyone else and could get away with murder in there 'cos I was the youngest.

The way you are constantly exposed is weird. You are in the shower and people are in the Jacuzzi watching you or maybe next to you cleaning the bathroom! Sleeping was easy, though, funnily enough. On the first

kenzie

Big Brother is evil

The way you are constantly
exposed is **weird**

kenzie

night, I thought, 'Please don't sleep talk and say anything stupid,' but I slept like a baby. Every time I snored Jeremy would wake me up and hold my nose! Jeremy, Bez and Brigitte found it really quite hard to sleep, but I was out like a light every night.

On the final night, when they said, 'Kenzie, you are second', I was just,

'Right, sweet, get me out of here!'

The crowd went mad; they were screaming and there was so much love for me out there. I did an interview with Davina and the audience were laughing at what I said. I was entertaining people and it was wicked. Then I saw my mum and dad come in and I just went for them, I was crying, man! I hugged 'em and grabbed 'em for about a minute, then all the Blazin' boys, Albert, Dave and Amy came over, I was so emotional about seeing everyone and they said, 'You've done yourself proud!'

I got back to my room to freshen up and sat down with Dave, but I was just shaking so I smoked two cigarettes then drank a whole bottle of red wine in about ten minutes flat. Then I got my phones back … aaahh! Then it was straight into a press conference with all these tabloids firing questions at me and I couldn't help thinking, 'You didn't care about me a month ago!' They were all asking about me going solo but this woman from *Big Brother* stepped in and said they shouldn't be going down that road. Chris Moyles' person was there from Radio 1 saying Chris had supported me on his show and I thought, 'Chris Moyles hates Blazin' Squad.' I listened to this guy and said, 'Tell him I said sweet.' Do you know what I mean?

When I finally got to the green room, I was starting to relax a little. It was filled with contestants, family and supporters. I was starting to get a little drunk and cheeky so I put my arm around one of the waitresses and was like, 'Hello, darling, what's your name?'

This bloke working behind the bar came up to me and said, 'I wouldn't go there, mate. She's only sixteen.'

I said, 'Look, I'm only nineteen, innit!'

She walked off and I said to him, 'She's a bit tasty, isn't she?'

He was looking a little funnily at me and seemed to be saying just tread carefully.

I said, 'No worries, man, I've got it in the bag, I've got it on lock, she's giving me free drinks and everything, I got her number and everything!'

He leaned over to me and said, 'Oh yeah? That's my daughter.'

There was a long pause.

'Well, she's a really nice girl and in a few years, I will call her …'

new releases

It was only eighteen days in the **Big Brother** house but it was surprisingly tough. Anyone who has ever done it, I admire and respect unbelievably. Anyone who is thinking of doing the normal show, I would say to them, 'Don't! Don't ever do it, no way.' That's over two months. I was in there for two and a half weeks; that's a long holiday in Spain! Two months – oh my God! I wouldn't advise it, I really wouldn't, but some people just want to be famous.

To someone whose career is in the public eye anyway, I would recommend it, yes. I did it for the profile. I didn't do it for the wages; it was nice to get that, but I did it for the profile. The amount it has done for me I would have done that show for free, God's honest truth. What it has done for me is out of this world, incredible!

I didn't hit my pillow until early the next morning, after more interviews and some time with my mum. A few hours later some of my boys slapped the papers in front of me and said, 'Have a go! See what they are saying.' I flicked quickly through all the papers thinking, 'What if they say I am a prick?', but there wasn't one single bad word about me. I got no slatings at all. It was just pure positive energy. What a touch! The funniest thing was, I saw this boy in the photos and I just looked like a child compared to everyone else; it didn't really hit home it was me until about a week later. But by then, complete madness had broken loose.

Then the phone rang.

'Hey, Kenzie. Morning. Do you want to go on Richard & Judy?'

It hit me quite hard when I came out of the house and found myself all over the tabloids. It was all very positive, don't get me wrong, but it was just not something I was used to. In Blazin' Squad I was lucky enough to be one of the band the magazines would often put on the front cover. I would talk a lot in interviews and always had the confidence to step up on stage too. But even though I was used to doing my own interviews and photo shoots, it was never as extreme as this. After *Big Brother*, I was in the tabloids every day and I am not used to that. So that was a shock. TV is a powerful thing. I did that *Richard & Judy* and all these TV shows and within days my schedule

was booked up for months ahead – two or three PAs
a night, interviews all day, *Top of the Pops*, everything;
it just went mad.

I had a big party for coming out of *Big Brother* and
a belated birthday party at a place called Sugar Hut in
Brentwood. It was my first proper piss-up after the house.
My boys were all there, quite a few were suited and
booted, there were loads of girls there. Gary got us all
this champagne. It was just the maddest night ever. It was
great to see all the boys and all my other mates outside
the band.

When I left the house, though, I wasn't eating well,
or sleeping for more than four hours. I didn't know what
was going on in my life so it was odd. I am so young
and it was a lot to take on board. So at first it was very
weird, but once I got used to it I was full steam ahead,
constantly shattered but loving life!

I would never complain about my job because I feel very lucky to be doing what I'm doing. Mind you, some days it would be nice to be able to sleep! I'll give you an example of one of my hardest days: it makes me laugh now thinking about how exhausted I was.

I did a PA the night before and got back to my room at 1.00 a.m. The next morning at 5.00 a.m I was being picked up by a car, so my alarm went off at 4.00 a.m. I got ready and headed out to film a TV show called *Celebrities Under Pressure*. The car took me to the airport and I got on a plane to Manchester. I'd already been working like a nutter since the *Big Brother* house so by 8.00 a.m I was feeling it. I fell into the back of another car to take me to Ramsbottom, Bury, near Manchester, and in the back I was trying to swig back coffee, hallucinating from the caffeine rush and the exhaustion.

I had to do these shots of me walking up to this family's house; they lived in this narrow, freezing cold windswept street and we had to keep shooting it to get it right. I met the family, who were lovely, then I was taken to find out what task I was doing – rock climbing! By midday, I had some lunch then had to climb up a wall for four hours. I got back to my room then had to pretend to go to the cinema (for the programme), then it was straight into a few radio interviews at local stations.

I got back to the family's house really late and had a glass of white wine at 1.00 a.m, having been up for twenty-one hours. Then I finally rolled into bed about 2.00 a.m and was up again at 7.00 a.m to go to a fire station to abseil down a seventy-foot fire tower, clipping dummy babies on to my belt as I went! Then, to finish me off, I had to do a fitness workout with these massive firemen! The very next day I did a PA in Reading around 6.00 p.m, then we had to drive to Newport, two hours each way, for another PA, then I got back in the car to be told we had yet another PA ... back in Reading! And it was only round the corner from the first one!

The thing is, when you get tired like this, you can't have people seeing you not smiling, being depressed and not on top of your game. They want to see the boy who was entertaining in the *Big Brother* house; they don't care if you've had a long day, and, really, why should they?

Doing a PA on your own can be quite intimidating, especially at first. Remember, I am used to there being ten of us wherever we go. Plus, every Blazin' Squad PA was for under-eighteens. Once I was out of the house, I was booked for dozens of PAs on my own, all over-eighteens, so naturally I was pretty apprehensive. The first one was Yates's in Romford. I was with Mark Sutton, my new tour manager, sitting in Pizza Hut and I just said, 'Mark, I am not doing it, I am too worried. They are going to take the piss out of me, there will be no love in there at all for me; sorry, bruv, forget the money, I can't do it.'

Mark was very cool about it and said, 'Just trust me!' I went in there and … oh my God! Within about ten minutes they had me judging this pole-dancing competition. I was on the mike chatting with the boys about these girls, the women were all screaming at me, it was a totally different experience from what I expected! I had a few drinks and then said I was going upstairs if anyone was interested, then when I got there the upstairs room was rammed, these snaking long queues waiting for my autograph, as many boys as girls. It was unreal. I've had such a great time doing these PAs, and now I am really confident and love them.

We stayed in Newcastle for another PA and word had got round so there were loads of girls there; it got a little crazy. We had a great night, sank forty-five shots between us and got proper battered, which I hadn't done for a long time. The next morning, I got out of bed and looked out of the window and the hotel was surrounded by police. They were everywhere. I thought, 'Well, a few of the girls got out of hand, but I don't remember it being that bad!' Then I found out that Tony Blair was staying there too, which was a relief!

When I ask for a glass of wine at these bars, because of *Big Brother* they always say, 'Do you want a straw with that?' I like to stand at the bar and have a drink and a chat. You can see people thinking, 'He ain't sipping champagne giving everyone dirty looks; he's doing free shots at the bar, getting battered and trying to chat up a girl! That's real!' I sign more autographs for housewives now than anyone else. Someone came up to me the other day and said, 'Oh, will you speak to

my niece?' so I got on
the phone and said, 'Hiya!
How ya doin'?' and she said, 'I'm
twenty-six!' I did a meet-and-greet with a fifty-
year-old woman and she was like, 'I love you!',
and I thought, 'But aren't you a nan?' Aspects of post-*Big
Brother* are so different from Blazin' Squad. For example,
boys come up to me asking me to sign stuff for their
girlfriends, whereas before the boyfriends generally hated
us and made it quite clear. If I get a younger boy who is still
insecure about it all, I just find out which one is his girlfriend
and blow her kisses, just to wind him up. I shouldn't really,
but sometimes I can't help myself!

I have a new team around me on the road now, which
is exciting. Mark Sutton is more like a big brother (sorry)
than a workmate. He works with Tony Cave, who has been
involved with big people before (such as the Beckhams and
Oasis). When we walk in somewhere with them it looks
proper, real professional. It's a fresh start for us and I like
that. Mind you, they have their work cut out looking after
things! One time we went to Derry and did a weekend
with Mark and Tony and ran up a £2,800 bar bill in two
nights. One night we consumed eighty-six shots; every
single member of the band, plus Mark and Tony, was sick

in their room. We all left our rooms the next morning with pillowcases full of sick and the entire floor of the hotel just stank of sick.

One thing I am determined to do is keep my feet on the ground. You get all this adulation and attention and you do see people beginning to believe their own hype. You hear stuff like, 'Where's my grapes? I want my grapes peeled!', and I think 'Get over yourself!' I hate all that.

I also hate sitting in the corner of some VIP area of a club sipping champagne. I'd much rather walk round with a JD and Coke and my mates chatting to girls any day! I understand some celebrities need to do that for security reasons, but I don't like it myself. That said, sometimes people can get a bit lairy and I have to be careful. I need my face; I can't have two black eyes when I turn up for *TRL* or *Top of the Pops*!

Living with my parents helps me keep things real. Kids in the street come up to me and say, 'How many millions you got then, mate?' If they only knew! When people say they are surprised I live with my mum and dad, I say, 'Yeah, that's me. That's real. If I really wanted to move out I could but that's not what I am about.' I am looked after there, I get all the love there, I just don't see the point; besides, all my real friends say don't leave home too early.

The boys in Blazin' Squad keep my feet on the ground too; they will never let me become a diva. But there is another group of mates who are not involved in the music business at all who are vital to me keeping it real. People like Joe Graham (Ging), Josh (the first mate I ever met; he taught me how to roller-skate), Tom Holmes (nickname Egg, but I can't call him that any more after my *Big Brother* fancy dress disaster!), Richie 'the Warrior', Mark Cumber, Will Beswick (nickname Bez, but we can't call him that any more either!). They are electricians and tradesmen and they've known me since I was a kid, so they won't put up with any diva behaviour either.

Late in 2004 I actually went out to work for a day with Beswick. They were taking the mickey out of me and my line of work and I said, 'All right, I'll come to work

kenzie

for you!' And I did. I was in this house pulling out wires, smashing plaster up and all that, but I tell you what: I was shattered. At the end of the day I said, 'There's no way I'm doing that again!'

These are my boys. I take 'em with me on the road sometimes; we book out two rooms and go on nights out. In the West End I introduce them to club owners so they know them and we have a great time. I want to give a little back to them because they look after me when I go out. The funny thing is, they have learnt a lot about tour managing from when we go out – one night my mate was at a gig with me and I overheard him saying, 'All right, line up, girls, get everything ready that you want signed …' He was proper busy, organizing it. It was hilarious!

I miss them a lot when I can't be around. They keep me level-headed. They give different opinions; it's all good. I ain't even famous to them, it's great. I'd be lost without them.

So that's my journey so far. Blocks of ice through the roof, garage parties, pirate radio, recording studios, Number 1 singles, sell-out tours, **Big Brother**, **Richard & Judy** … and Sylvester Stallone's mum. Looking at it now, I can't believe how much has been crammed into so few years. And do you know what? I've loved all of it! Who knows what I am going to do next? I signed a record deal at sixteen, played Wembley at eighteen, then came second in **Celebrity Big Brother** at nineteen, so, for me, I think anything is possible!

kenzie